D0571586

BACK TO
JOY

BACK TO
JOY

Little Reminders to Help Us through Tough Times

June Cotner

Andrews McMeel Publishing

Kansas City • Sydney • London

BACK TO JOY

Andrews McMeel Publishing, LLC
an Andrews McMeel Universal company
1130 Walnut Street, Kansas City, Missouri 64106

www.andrewsmcmeel.com

Illustration by Josephine Kimberling

15 16 17 18 19 WKT 10 9 8 7 6 5 4 3 2

ISBN: 978-1-4494-4164-7

Library of Congress Control Number: 2014937596

ATTENTION: SCHOOLS AND BUSINESSES

Andrews McMeel books are available at quantity discounts with
bulk purchase for educational, business, or sales promotional use.
For information, please e-mail the Andrews McMeel Publishing
Special Sales Department: specialsales@amuniversal.com.

For Laura Jean Judson—
who always seeks joy in her life!

Do not wait for life.
Do not long for it.
Be aware, always and at every moment,
that the miracle is in the here and now.

— MARCEL PROUST

CONTENTS

eleven
GOOD LITTLE REMINDERS 159

LETTER TO READERS

The idea for this book blossomed from looking for a way to remind individuals that our lives have challenges and hard days, but that despite those hurdles, the good (and the great!) is still there. When we feel stuck or have temporarily lost our way, sometimes we need a reaffirmation to remind ourselves that we are still capable of making the changes in life that will result in finding joy again. It's not about letting life happen to you, or putting it out of your hands—it's about taking the reins and reminding yourself that pity-parties aren't any fun.

The purpose of *Back to Joy* is to provide positive reminders to people who tend to be happy, but may be struggling to enjoy life due to challenging circumstances. A reader can turn to any page in *Back to Joy* when he or she is feeling blue and read something that reminds one to think positively, refocus, and remember that "this too shall pass."

We all have people in our lives who need these gentle reminders—and we ourselves do, too, from time to time. When someone is going through a rough time in his or her life, it's nice to be able to turn to an inspirational quote, or a piece of text, which has a motivational message, something which can prod the person into remembering that it's not all bad and that joy could be around the corner.

Back to Joy is separated into chapters which loosely address the stages of an individual's journey through personal struggle, or just a bad day, back to the joy that is his or her natural state. These chapter headings include themes such as When Challenges Arise, Stamina and Faith, Taking the Reins, Finding Your Way, and Good Little Reminders. A reader can open the book to any section and find words that inspire us to take a deep breath and carry on. The messages in this book are the expression of how capable, courageous, and strong you can be.

I have been compiling anthologies for over 20 years and have more than 900 contributors who send me their poems, prayers, and prose for each of my books. Selecting just 300 pieces from the thousands considered for this book was an enormous challenge.

I had close to one thousand pieces that I loved, so it was difficult to whittle down the selections to the "best of the best."

While *Back to Joy* is a combination of classic words as well as new content, I hope this book will give you the solace and encouragement of some old friends saying to you, "Hey, it's OK. Don't worry about it so much. Look at all the great things in your life, and in the world. Things will get better, and really it's up to you to make it happen. Because you *can*."

May the selections in *Back to Joy* encourage you to return to the joy you have felt in the past—and discover even more joy in the present.

> June Cotner
> P.O. Box 2765
> Poulsbo, WA 98370
> june@junecotner.com
> www.junecotner.com

THANKS

My biggest thank you is to Laura Jean Judson, to whom this book is dedicated. We have worked together for about 10 years, and she is familiar with all of my books. While working on one of my newer projects, she said she thought a book that would offer hope, encouragement, and perspective to people who are going through tough times would be really valuable. And she was right. I had a tremendous outpouring of submissions on the topic of finding your way back to joy.

My two agents, Denise Marcil and Anne Marie O'Farrell, at Marcil—O'Farrell Literary, were both excited about the project, and so was my long-time editor, Patty Rice, at Andrews McMeel Publishing. I so appreciate the guidance, enthusiasm, and creativity of all three of you!

My heartfelt gratitude goes to my husband, Jim Graves, and my many relatives and friends who encourage and inspire me every day.

Much appreciation goes to the contributors of my books. Your words enrich my life in countless ways. Even for the poems and prose that don't make it into the final manuscript, your writing comes back to me in many delightful ways in my everyday life. I'm inspired to create future anthologies so others can enjoy your writing and have their lives graced by your perspectives.

And to God, I'm thankful for giving me a career that I love. I live with great appreciation of all the blessings in my life.

one

Normally Happy, But...

Every soul is a melody
which needs renewing.

—STÉPHANE MALLARMÉ

ROAD BACK TO JOY

Somewhere you lost your way. You were happy once, but circumstances took you on a detour. You're overwhelmed by massive roadblocks or unexpected potholes. You've been downsized—financially, emotionally, and/or physically.

If it's any comfort, most of the people you know are suffering, too. Many lives have been rudely adjusted to a world we didn't envision, plan, or create. Recovery or getting by might be your "new normal."

Despite your stalled momentum, there is a way back to joy. "Joy" is a simple word, refreshing as a breath of air. It conveys moments of pure pleasure. As a child you focused on small delights—running outdoors on the grass. A cup of hot chocolate. Watching a favorite movie over and over. A treasured stuffed animal. Sharing a secret.

Recall how you marveled at the things that brought you joy as you grew older. Children's laughter. Plunging into cool water and resurfacing. Sleeping late. Cracking open a new book. Flea markets. A breathtaking sunset.

You have problems to resolve, but you still have the capacity for joy. Rejoice in the things that give you pleasure now. Breathe. Enjoy a cup of calming tea or a bracing mug of coffee. Put your feet up. Let your hair down.

These small graces are momentary rest stops on the journey, but sometimes taking a break from a worry rut leads to a different path. What fun is a road trip without diversions? And sometimes a new direction is what you need to get back on the road to random joy.

⌐ MARY KOLADA SCOTT

THE JOURNEY

Without words, it comes. And suddenly, sharply, one is aware of being separated from every person on one's earth and every object, and from the beginning of things and from the future and even a little, from one's self. A moment before one was happily playing; the world was round and friendly. Now at one's feet there are chasms that had been invisible until this moment. And one knows, and never remembers how it was learned, that there will always be chasms, and across the chasms will always be those one loves.

⮑ LILLIAN SMITH

REBIRTH

When life's trials weigh you down like snow on a limb,
When strife steals your smile and your candle grows
    dim.

Like the branch of the tree, you're sure you will break,
You feel yourself falling, you think it's too late.

Just remember, with time the snow changes to rain,
And a smile will caress your lips once again.

The sun without warning will burst through the
    clouds,
Melt the snow from the branch with its radiant shroud.

And despite all life's sorrow, despite all its pain,
You emerge even stronger, you're whole once again.

⌒ BARB MAYER

FACING LIFE'S CHALLENGES

Sooner or later we will come to the edge of all that
we cannot control and find life, waiting there for us.

~ RACHEL NAOMI REMEN

There are better things ahead than any we
leave behind.

~ C.S. LEWIS

When you're going through hell, keep going.

~ WINSTON CHURCHILL

It's one short step from "why me" to "woe is me."

~ JOHN C. MAXWELL

If it weren't for the rocks in its bed, the stream
would have no song.

~ CARL PERKINS

When life's problems seem overwhelming, look around and see what other people are coping with. You may consider yourself fortunate.

꙰ ANN LANDERS

Your present circumstances don't determine where you can go; they merely determine where you start.

꙰ NIDO QUBEIN

Life is not meant to be easy, my child; but take courage—it can be delightful.

꙰ GEORGE BERNARD SHAW

BEGIN

Begin on the path, even if it winds.
Even if you do not know at first where it is going
and if it appears as a maze, a puzzle, a
   bewilderment.

The geese that fly south in winter,
north in spring, know their journey innately,
yet still use the stars to guide them.

Follow your very own star.
The one you have always wished upon.
You *can* find your way home.

∼ JEAN NICOLE BASS

two

When Challenges Arise

See every difficulty as a challenge,
a stepping stone, and never be
defeated by anything or anyone.

—EILEEN CADDY

RELAX

Bad things are going to happen.
Your tomatoes will grow a fungus
and your cat will get run over.
Someone will leave the bag with the ice cream
melting in the car and throw
your blue cashmere sweater in the dryer.
Your husband will sleep
with a girl your daughter's age, her breasts spilling
out of her blouse. Or your wife
will remember she's a lesbian
and leave you for the woman next door. The other
    cat—
the one you never really liked—will contract a
    disease
that requires you to pry open its feverish mouth
every four hours. Your parents will die.
No matter how many vitamins you take,
how much Pilates, you'll lose your keys,
your hair and your memory. If your daughter
doesn't plug her heart
into every live socket she passes,
you'll come home to find your son has emptied

the refrigerator, dragged it to the curb,
and called the used-appliance store for a pick up—
    drug money.
The Buddha tells a story of a woman chased by a
    tiger.
When she comes to a cliff, she sees a sturdy vine
and climbs half way down. But there's also a tiger
    below.
And two mice—one white, one black—scurry out
and begin to gnaw at the vine. At this point
she notices a wild strawberry growing from a
    crevice.
She looks up, down, at the mice.
Then she eats the strawberry.
So here's the view, the breeze, the pulse
in your throat. Your wallet will be stolen, you'll get
    fat,
slip on the bathroom tiles in a foreign hotel
and crack your hip. You'll be lonely.
Oh taste how sweet and tart
the red juice is, how the tiny seeds
crunch between your teeth.

⎉ ELLEN BASS

PERMISSION GRANTED

Why is it that we never feel entitled,
To take care of ourselves,
When we most need care?
Even the storm takes care of itself,
Raining until there is no more rain,
Not asking anyone's permission,
To light up the sky, fill the gutters, and leak into the
   kitchen.
A storm has come into your life, wreaking havoc
   and chaos,
And you're the one needing permission?
You have it:
Permission to feel afraid, but not feel conquered by
   your fears,
Permission to feel overwhelmed, but not undone,
Permission to pause, shed a few tears, take a breath,
Permission to sit with a cup of coffee and find the
   still center of yourself—
In the eye of the storm—

where all your strength lies in waiting.
Storms come and pass, and you are stronger
   because of them.
It's stormy now.
You have permission to feel the power of the storm,
and seek the shelter within yourself.

∽— SUSAN KOEFOD

PERSPECTIVE

Difficult times have helped me to understand better than before how infinitely rich and beautiful life is in every way, and that so many things that one goes worrying about are of no importance whatsoever.

⌒ ISAK DINESEN

If you focus on what you left behind, you will never be able to see what lies ahead.

⌒ GUSTEAU, *RATATOUILLE*

If we all threw our problems in a pile and saw everyone else's, we'd grab ours back.

⌒ REGINA BRETT

The years teach much which the days never knew.

⌒ RALPH WALDO EMERSON

WHEN CHALLENGES ARISE

We cannot choose our external circumstances, but we can always choose how we respond to them.

⌀— EPICTETUS

If you worry about what might be, and wonder what might have been, you will ignore what is.

⌀— AUTHOR UNKNOWN

Worry never robs tomorrow of its sorrow; it only saps today of its joy.

⌀— LEO BUSCAGLIA

What does not destroy me, makes me stronger.

⌀— FRIEDRICH NIETZSCHE

EMBRACE UNCERTAINTY AS A CLOUD

When uncertainty hangs humid
   Thick as a steel-gray sky
And you can't tell if a storm hovers
   In the charcoal clouds
Or if only a gentle Zen rain will follow,
   Return to that still, quiet place.
Imagine you are the water itself,
   The deep center of a blue, glacial lake,
The sizzling tide pulled back to its source.
   Know that whatever rain must come
Has its purpose if you wish to find it.
   The rain takes many forms, gathering
Its legions with the wind, which might be
   Sweet spring breezes or wind sheer
Pulling pines and locusts from their roots.
   Embrace uncertainty as a cloud holding water,
Building its cumulous castles in the stratosphere,
   Until release comes, and come it will.

     CHRISTINE SWANBERG

SOMETIMES WE MUST LET THE WEEPING COME,

to bring its soft relief
like a dry summer's rain;
a small brook flowing
amid the reaching ferns.

Sometimes to confess
the sadness we've been holding
makes way for a lightness again,
or at least the hint of an opening.

If the heart, like a cup, is too full,
we must spill some sorrows out—
to make room for the possible gift
of something new, or fresh, or healing.

༄ INGRID GOFF-MAIDOFF

ADVERSITY

If we had no winter, the spring would not be so
pleasant; if we did not sometimes taste of adversity,
prosperity would not be so welcome.

— ANNE BRADSTREET

The most beautiful people we have known are
those who have known defeat, known suffering,
known struggle, known loss, and have found their
way out of the depths. These persons have an
appreciation, a sensitivity, and an understanding of
life that fills them with compassion, gentleness, and
a deep loving concern. Beautiful people do not just
happen.

— ELISABETH KÜBLER-ROSS

The flower that blooms in adversity is the most rare
and beautiful of all.

— THE EMPEROR, *MULAN*

WHEN LIFE TAKES GUTS

When someone says, "That took guts,"
you should be able to
bare the memory and show the scar you carry.
"Yes—here is where life took guts,
and here,
and here,
and here.
And I have survived."

∾ LAURA BYRNES

TO LIVE WITH AN OPEN HEART

It is only through letting our heart break that we discover something unexpected: the heart cannot actually break, it can only break open. When we feel both our love for this world and the pain of this world—together, at the same time—the heart breaks out of its shell. To live with an open heart is to experience life full-strength.

— JOHN WELWOOD

DIFFICULTIES

Real difficulties can be overcome; it is only the imaginary ones that are unconquerable.

⌐ THEODORE N. VAIL

A pessimist sees the difficulty in every opportunity; an optimist sees the opportunity in every difficulty.

⌐ WINSTON CHURCHILL

Setbacks are given to ordinary people to make them extraordinary.

⌐ PAUL JEFFERS

Sometimes your struggles become your expertise.

⌐ LAUREN KATE CIMINERA

A FAILURE

Often a notable failure serves the world as faithfully as a distinguished success. As a tree is fertilized by its own broken branches and fallen leaves, so great souls use their own failures, and convert them to useful ends. . . . A failure may be a blessing in disguise. It may mean a new direction for our lives.

⌒ DALE TURNER

GRADUAL HEALING

[An] emphasis on gradual healing should apply even when we are not mourning the loss of a life. A divorce is a form of death. It's the death of a dream, of a love, and of a life together. Losing a job is also a death of our sense of security, of our income, lifestyle, status, and identity. A serious illness can be a death. It's the loss of our health, of our strength, of our confidence in our own bodies. *Every* pain takes time to heal.

⌒ NAOMI LEVY

THREE WORDS

I can sum up everything
I've learned about life:
it goes on.

~ ROBERT FROST

three

It Will Get Better

What wound did ever heal
but by degrees?

—WILLIAM SHAKESPEARE

BETTER TIMES AHEAD

Every exit is an entry somewhere else.

⌒ TOM STOPPARD

If you can remember how you thought you would
never survive that struggle you faced before, you
could be just as wrong about the outcome of the
situation you are dealing with today.

⌒ JILL N. MACGREGOR

When you get into a tight place and everything
goes against you until it seems that you cannot hold
on for a minute longer, never give up then, for that
is just the place and time when the tide will turn.

⌒ HARRIET BEECHER STOWE

Your dreams still exist even if a storm surrounds
you. A safe harbor is coming.

⌒ JUNE COTNER

STEADFAST HOPE

Out of times
of tremendous trial
sprout seasons
of abundant growth.

— JOAN MARIE ARBOGAST

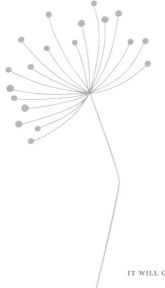

JUST

when you feel you're crawling
through the darkest night
that wraps you in its burning ice
and you're afraid the endless night
will swallow you,
just keep on,
inch by slow inch,
for one day dawn will break
and you'll dance
embracing warmth
and golden light.

~ RUTH FOGELMAN

HOPE

Hope begins in the dark, the stubborn hope that if you just show up and try to do the right thing, the dawn will come. You wait and watch and work; you don't give up.

∽ ANNE LAMOTT

The way to faith starts with a flickering candle. Let a little light lead the way.

∽ JUNE COTNER

Even when the friendly lights go out, there will be a light by which your heart sees.

∽ OLGA ROSMANITH

If you have forgotten what Hope is, Spend five minutes with a child.

∽ CORRINE DE WINTER

JUST BREATHE

I'd heard the expression for years:
JUST BREATHE.
Big deal. So what. Platitude. Simplistic.
I didn't get it
(and I also didn't give it much thought).
And then one December, my father was sick.
Really sick.
On his fourth hospital stay.
Throw in unexpected company
and quickly approaching Christmas
with its trappings (or should I say traipsing,
in a hundred different directions
on holiday errands).
I was opening the car door
after finishing another errand.
If I could have sunk through the parking lot
to the center of the earth and stayed there,
I might have.
I remember holding
onto the door handle for a second.

"Breathe," a voice from within instructed.
"Stand still and breathe."
I did.
And then I got it.
JUST BREATHE!
Sometimes, standing still and breathing
is just what you need to do.
Sometimes, at least in that moment,
it's all you can do.
But small miracles abound in those breaths.
Almost always,
they fuel the courage to go on.

⌒ BARBARA YOUNGER

BREATHING BETWEEN THE LINES

Life is not always a straight line
but if you follow each turn and stay on course
you can be certain the path you chose
is the one you are meant to follow.

Close your eyes and listen to the world.
There are answers in the stillness
and around each corner you can embrace
the quiet gifts that life has to offer.

So as you journey through your life,
embrace each chapter with the knowledge
that you are headed in the right direction.
And as you share your gifts with the world,
they will be celebrated as a reflection of the choices
you have made that bring you alive.

There is life to breathe between every verse
and through each uneven line.
Take comfort in knowing
that you are in the right place,
and that your life will be a significant expression
of the person you are meant to be.

Open your eyes and see your world.
You have the freedom to be something beautiful
so welcome all that is extraordinary around you.

⌒ LORI EBERHARDY

GREAT EXPECTATIONS

At times it is hard to see the light
through these shadows of doubt,
but there is hope in my soul.

With great expectations I reach past
the shadows that surround me.
I transcend the darkness and my spirit
becomes woven in the sunlight.

With tenderness I listen to the sweet
sounds of amazing grace,
and with the vision of a child,
I remind myself that
this is the day, the hour, the moment
to keep the faith.

— LORI EBERHARDY

FIND THE BEST IN ANYTHING

Always remind yourself:
You can find the best in anything.
Even with bad days,
a sparkle of gold glimmers
over the horizon of tomorrow.

⌒ JUNE COTNER

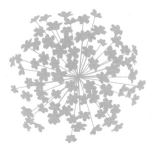

READY OR NOT . . .

Sometimes Life beckons – *It's time to move on* –
and we find ourselves gathering memories
of a lifetime, packing them into boxes
too few to hold them, and
whispering goodbyes
to rooms we've
known as Home.
Through tears
we trudge to
Somewhere New,
clinging to the past,
fearing the unknown,
and praying for
Strength to carry
our burdens.
Hesitant,
we arrive, climb
step after step, unlock
the front door, and sigh with
relief when Hope is there to greet us.

⌒ JOAN MARIE ARBOGAST

TROUBLES LIKE WEEDS

fill my battered garden
after a bitter winter.

Armed with shears
and heavy gloves
I yank and chop

but troubles have deep
taproots, resist my best
efforts. Then in the high
grass I discover

a golden iris, swaying
in the warm breeze.

⌁ ARLENE L. MANDELL

JUST OVER YONDER

J   O   Y

Stands for

Just
Over
Yonder

Sometimes
You have to wait
For the yonder
Just a bit longer,
As green shoots sprout
Into fields of joy.

⌒ BARBARA YOUNGER

FINISH EVERY DAY

Finish every day and be done with it. You have done what you could. Some blunders and absurdities no doubt have crept in; forget them as soon as you can. Tomorrow is a new day; begin it well and serenely and with too high a spirit to be cumbered with your old nonsense. This day is all that is good and fair. It is too dear, with its hopes and invitations, to waste a moment on yesterdays.

⌒ RALPH WALDO EMERSON

BE STRONG

Be strong,
be brave, be true.
Endure.

⌐ DAVE EGGERS

four

Stamina and Faith

Faith is the bird that feels the light
and sings when the dawn is still dark.

—RABINDRANATH TAGORE

YOUR STRENGTH

The human spirit is stronger than anything that
can happen to it.

— GEORGE C. SCOTT

We never have more than we can bear. The present
hour we are always able to endure. As is our day,
so is our strength. If the trials of many years were
gathered into one, they would overwhelm us . . .
but all is so wisely measured to our strength that the
bruised reed is never broken.

— H. E. MANNING

God does not take away trials or carry us over
them, but strengthens us through them.

— E. B. PUSEY

You are braver than you believe,
and stronger than you seem,
and smarter than you think.

— A. A. MILNE
EXCERPT FROM *WINNIE THE POOH*

VAILIMA PRAYER

Give us grace and strength
to forbear and to persevere.
Give us courage and gaiety
and the quiet mind.
Spare to us our friends, soften
to us our enemies. Bless us
if it may be in all our
innocent endeavors. If it
may not, give us the strength
to encounter that which is to
come, that we may be brave
in peril, constant in tribulation,
temperate in wrath.
And in all changes of fortune
And down to the gates of death
Loyal and loving
To one another.

⌒ ROBERT LOUIS STEVENSON

COURAGE

The greatest test of courage on earth is to bear
defeat without losing heart.

      ⌐ ROBERT G. INGERSOLL

Shower me with courage to see
real gifts seldom come in square boxes.

      ⌐ NANCY TUPPER LING

Let us not pray to be sheltered from dangers but to
be fearless when facing them.

      ⌐ RABINDRANATH TAGORE

Be strong and of good courage;
do not be afraid, nor be dismayed.

      ⌐ JOSHUA 1:9 (NKJV)

ON SORROW

Where there is sorrow there is holy ground.

⌒ OSCAR WILDE

Crisis can force us deep enough to find that source of passion in whatever you truly love. The deeper the channel that pain carves into our soul, the greater the capacity we have to allow the river of joy to run through us.

⌒ DAWNA MARKOVA

Every life has a measure of sorrow. Sometimes it is this that awakens us.

⌒ ANCIENT BUDDHIST SAYING

Have courage for the great sorrows of life, and patience for the small ones. When you have laboriously accomplished your daily tasks, go to sleep in peace. God is awake.

⌒ VICTOR HUGO

THE SUN'S TOUCH

Shadow of grief
A fog dulling my senses,
Days blur together
Automatic pilot takes over.
I step into a patch of sunlight,
The warmth kisses my face
I close my eyes
And let the incandescence seep in
Just a tiny bit,
A reminder that I can still feel—
When I am ready, I will embrace the sun again.

◦— NANCY ENGLER

CONFIDENCE

It's always within yourself
that you find the strength
to dance the steps you've dreamed.

∽ LAURA JEAN JUDSON

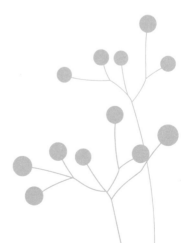

ON SUFFERING

Out of suffering have emerged the strongest of souls.

— KHALIL GIBRAN

Although the world is full of suffering, it is also full of the overcoming of it.

— HELEN KELLER

I do not believe that sheer suffering teaches. If suffering alone taught, all the world would be wise, since everyone suffers. To suffering must be added mourning, understanding, patience, love, openness, and the willingness to remain vulnerable.

— ANNE MORROW LINDBERGH

Though much is taken, much abides . . .

— ALFRED, LORD TENNYSON

FAITH

The wind blows wherever it pleases. You hear its sound,
but you cannot tell where it comes from or where it
is going. — JOHN 3:8 (NIV)

Sometimes the wind blows and
sometimes it doesn't—

Sometimes we have warning of
the hurricane at our doorstep and
sometimes the furniture slams us
to the floor, leaving us bruised,
dazed, and wounded—

Sometimes the wind fills our sails
and we dance across deep waters with
our hair streaming, safe harbor in sight and
sometimes we languish in breathless
doldrums, our sails empty and limp
as our faith—

For who can predict the wind, where
it will go and when it will come; a
fool chases after what he cannot predict,
but a wise man waits with his hand
on the rudder for the next
irrational
breath of the Almighty.

⌐ SALLY CLARK

IN DARKNESS

Bless my time in darkness
that it may simply be
a waiting within
a chrysalis.

And I will emerge
anew
with the warmth of the sun
to dry my wings.

⌒ BARBARA DAVIS-PYLES

FAITH SUSTAINS

Faith is taking the first step even when you don't see the whole staircase.

— MARTIN LUTHER KING, JR.

I have learned that faith means trusting in advance what will only make sense in reverse.

— PHILIP YANCEY

Faith is the assurance of things hoped for, the conviction of things not seen.

— HEBREWS 11:1 (RSV)

Sorrow looks back. Worry looks around. Faith looks ahead.

— BEATRICE FALLON

DIVINE GUIDANCE

I believe we are free, within limits, and yet there is
an unseen hand, a guiding angel, that somehow,
like a submerged propeller, drives us on.

⌒ RABINDRANATH TAGORE

We arrive precisely where we need to arrive
because the hand of God always guides those who
follow their path with faith.

⌒ PAULO COELHO

An inspired life is living deeply connected with the divine. . . . Miracles happen because our eyes are open to seeing them. Challenges become opportunities to evolve. Every moment carries the possibility for experiencing great joy.

~ LYNDRA HEARN ANTONSON

You are not a reservoir with a limited amount of resources; you are a channel attached to unlimited divine resources.

~ AUTHOR UNKNOWN

ANGELS

We each have a guardian angel
Blessed by the peace she brings
And although we cannot see her
We feel the brush of wings.
No heavenly clash of thunder,
Nor vision of golden throne,
Just faithful certitude
That we are not alone.
She brings us light in darkness,
Gives calm in times of fear;
Hope lives in the knowing
That she is always near.
Compassion for our tears,
Comfort with each nod;
Her mission is no chance of fate—
She is a gift from God.

⌒ C. DAVID HAY

PATIENCE

After sowing, there is a period of time when it looks like nothing is happening. All the growth is below the surface.

             ∽ NABI SALEH

The lowest ebb is the turn of the tide.

             ∽ HENRY WADSWORTH LONGFELLOW

In the midst of winter, I found there was, within me, an invincible summer.

             ∽ ALBERT CAMUS

Have patience with everything unresolved in your heart and try to love the questions themselves.

             ∽ RAINER MARIA RILKE

KEEP TRYING

When you have exhausted all possibilities,
remember this: you haven't.

⤙ THOMAS EDISON

We are what we repeatedly do. Excellence, then, is
not an act but a habit.

⤙ ARISTOTLE

Every day you must arise and say to your heart, "I
have suffered enough and now I must live because
the light of the sun must not be wasted, it must not
be lost without an eye to appreciate it."

⤙ SIMONE SCHWARZ-BART

Our greatest glory is not in never falling, but in
rising every time we fall.

⤙ CONFUCIUS

five

Making Changes

Each step is the journey;
a single note the song.

—ARLENE GAY LEVINE

MAKING CHANGES

Sometimes I lie awake at night, and I ask, "Where have I gone wrong?" Then a voice says to me, "This is going to take more than one night."

∽ CHARLES M. SCHULTZ

Tame your passions before making important decisions; good judgment is most likely to occur when the head is cool, the body is rested, and the stomach is full

∽ NORMAN E. ROSENTHAL

We must always change, renew, rejuvenate ourselves; otherwise we harden.

⟿ JOHANN WOLFGANG VON GOETHE

Throw your dream into space like a kite, and you do not know what it will bring back: a new life, a new friend, a new love, a new country.

⟿ ANAÏS NIN

CHOICES

Life is a sum of all your choices.

— ALBERT CAMUS

Every choice moves us closer to or farther away from something. Where are your choices taking your life? What do your behaviors demonstrate that you are saying yes or no to in life?

— ERIC ALLENBAUGH

Choice, not chance, determines your destiny. It's up to you to decide what you are worth, how you matter, and how you make meaning in the world. No one else has your gifts—your set of talents, ideas, interests. You are an original. A masterpiece.

⟡ REGINA BRETT

In the long run, we shape our lives and we shape ourselves. The process never ends until we die. And the choices we make are ultimately our responsibility.

⟡ ELEANOR ROOSEVELT

CHANGE YOURSELF

Change your thoughts and you change your world.

⌒ NORMAN VINCENT PEALE

Yesterday I was clever, so I wanted to change the world. Today I am wise, so I am changing myself.

⌒ RUMI

When we are no longer able to change a situation, we are challenged to change ourselves.

⌒ VIKTOR FRANKL

Whether you believe you can do a thing or not, you are right.

⌒ HENRY FORD

STRETCH YOURSELF

In contemplating a difficult path, remember that
many others have gone that way before you.
If they could succeed, then with a little hope,
resourcefulness, and help from others, the chances
are that you can too.

⟿ NORMAN E. ROSENTHAL

The greatest stretching seasons of life come when we
do what we have never done, push ourselves harder,
and reach in a way that is uncomfortable to us. That
takes courage. But the good news is that it causes us
to grow in ways we thought impossible. And it gives
life to what novelist George Eliot said: "It's never too
late to be what you might have been."

⟿ JOHN C. MAXWELL

If we want to solve a problem that we have never
solved before, we must leave the door to the
unknown ajar.

⟿ RICHARD P. FEYNMAN

SEND OUT SOME JOY

Send out some joy.
Balloons to the hospital.
Books to the flooded school.
Cookies to the security guard.
Pet food to the shelter.
Extra coins in the tip jar.
Send out some joy, and
Feel the joy come splashing back.

⌒ BARBARA YOUNGER

IF I HAD MY LIFE TO LIVE OVER

If I had my life to live over,
I would start barefoot earlier in the spring
and stay that way later in the fall.
I would go to more dances.
I would ride more merry-go-rounds.
I would pick more daisies.

⌒ NADINE STAIR

THE NEXT STEP

My life used to be like that game of freeze tag we played as kids. Once tagged, you had to freeze in the situation you are in. Whenever something happened, I'd freeze like a statue, too afraid of moving the wrong way, too afraid of making the wrong decision. The problem is, if you stand still too long, that's your decision. When in doubt, do the next right thing.

    ⁀ REGINA BRETT

Don't dwell on what went wrong. Instead, focus on what to do next. Spend your energies on moving forward toward finding the answer.

    ⁀ DENIS WAITLEY

If you keep doing what you've always done, you'll keep getting what you've always got.

⌒ PETER FRANCISCO

When you have a number of disagreeable duties to perform, always do the most disagreeable first.

⌒ JOSIAH QUINCY

SELF-EMBRACE

I take myself
into my arms

and rest there
when I am tired.

⌒ SUDIE NOSTRAND

SANCTUARY

There is a sanctuary in your heart
where the spirit always waits.

⌒ CORRINE DE WINTER

ATTENTION

Do not
leave your
longings
unattended.

⌒ AUSTIN KLEON

six

Taking the Reins

The journey is yours to make.
Leap!

—JUNE COTNER

START NOW

The first step towards getting somewhere is to decide that you are not going to stay where you are.

∽ J. P. MORGAN

Although no one can go back and make a brand new start, anyone can start now and make a brand new ending.

∽ CARL BARD

You cannot change your destination overnight, but you can change your direction overnight.

∽ JIM ROHN

Whatever you can do or dream you can, begin it. Boldness has genius, power and magic in it. Begin it now.

∽ JOHANN WOLFGANG VON GOETHE

The way to get started is to quit talking and begin doing.

Act boldly and unseen forces will come to your aid.

Don't wait for extraordinary opportunities. Seize common occasions and make them great.

Twenty years from now you will be more disappointed by the things you didn't do than by the ones you did. So, throw off the bowlines, sail away from the safe harbor, catch the trade winds in your sails. Explore. Dream. Discover.

LIFE IS MESSY

Rivers know this: there is no hurry.
We shall get there some day.

⌐ A.A. MILNE, *WINNIE-THE-POOH*

Life is messy, mixed up, and never a straight road.
Treat! Don't retreat. Go ahead. Take a long bubble
bath! Go for a walk. Reflect.

Go out to the garden. Remember sometimes you
must pull out the weeds before flowers can grow. Be
patient. Always keep the vision of what you want in
front of you. Work on it a bit every day. Remember,
it takes time to cultivate your field of dreams. And
one day, what seemed like a dirt road will be a road
full of flowers.

⌐ SHERRI WAAS SHUNFENTHAL

THE TREASURE

It is not found in books,
They are merely maps.

It is buried deep
In experience.

— JANINE CANAN

14 LITTLE WAYS TO BEAT THE BLUES

1. Don't even think of staying in bed.
2. Open a window. Say thanks for the day.
3. Skip grooming? Never!
4. Resolve to accomplish one thing today.
5. Spend time with nature: feed the birds, tend flowers, etc.
6. Call a friend just to chat.
7. Do something social. (Buying groceries qualifies.)
8. Ask a neighbor to go for a walk.
9. "Fluff" your house to look nice.
10. Do at least one thing you look forward to each day.
11. Say thank you at every opportunity.
12. Volunteer for something you enjoy.
13. Give compliments.
14. Know that every day contains a small miracle. Your job is to find it.

— DEMAR REGIER

BE KIND TO YOURSELF

Before the sun dips into the ocean,
Disappearing until dawn,
Catch the glow that warms your spirit.
Play a song that will soothe the pain.
Remember the vision of a gentle memory.
Be kind to yourself
So that you may have the strength
To get through tomorrow.
Be warmed by the sun, embrace the wind.
Hope, smile, find the grace within and be still,
If only to renew your faith for now.

— JUDITH A. LINDBERG

JUMP!

Whatever it is
That I think I am
I am that, and so much more
How many times do I limit myself
Thinking small
When life is large
Feigning weakness
When I have the strength to move mountains
Bowing low
When I should hold my head high
Coloring inside the lines
Fearing to step outside the box
Where all the wonders of life await
JUMP!

— NANCY LYNCH GIBSON

ELEVATOR STORY

I had gotten on the elevator, intending to go
to the 4th floor. Instead, it headed for the
basement. There were two others with me.
One said, "Sometimes you have to go down to
go up" and the other said, "At least you're on
the elevator."

— EDIE WEINSTEIN

FRIENDS INDEED

I tend to be shy about making friends. So when I heard about my neighbor, Ellie, and how she'd had knee replacement surgery, I wasn't sure if I should call her or not. After all, we'd never actually spoken. She was always working in her rose garden when I took my daily walk. She'd wave and say hi, and I'd smile and wave back, but that was the extent of it. After hearing the news, I knew she must be feeling pain along with disappointment because she couldn't go outdoors. I figured she probably had cabin fever since she couldn't dig in her garden.

After much hesitation, I looked up her number and dialed it. We chatted quite awhile and she seemed pleased to hear from me. She also was astonished that I called her, telling me over and over how nice it was to know someone cared.

Not long afterwards, I injured my back and was put on bed rest. Although Ellie had no knowledge of my injury, she spotted my husband one afternoon, invited him into her house, then asked him to present me with a breathtaking arrangement of roses. I wasn't happy about being laid up either, so her bouquet brought a big smile to my face.

Sometimes friendships never get off the ground. But a simple phone call or a bunch of flowers can stave off shyness, loneliness or whatever prevents us from taking that first step toward knowing someone. Ellie is back in her garden now and I've resumed my walks that take me by her house. We're both glad that good friendships last much longer than any kind of pain could!

— JILL FRANCES DAVIS

THE ART OF JOY

During his teens and early adulthood, my son did drugs and time. I despaired and tried everything to help—counseling, coaxing, bribing, and enabling. During one bleak period, I started attending a 12-step support group for families of addicts on Monday nights at the neighborhood church. I cried every Monday for a year listening to other heartbroken parents share similar stories of grief. One night, I realized that my son was out partying while I agonized over his lifestyle. He was having fun and I was miserable. I decided I wasn't helping him or me.

Instead, I enrolled in a watercolor class one night a week. It provided the focus I needed to move from obsessing about him to nurturing myself. I loved the challenge of learning and absorbing a fresh perspective and new language, such as "scumbling" and "fugitive color." I had a new group of supportive women who shared wise and funny insights on parenting. And it gave me a new life as an artist. Eventually, my son matured and got straight, got out of prison, got a job, and got married. My first grandchild was born the same year I had my first solo art show, and I was grateful to celebrate both. Some of my paintings hang in my son's home now, including portraits I've painted of my beautiful grandchildren. The greatest compliment I get from admirers is that they feel happy when they see my paintings—and I'm elated to share that joy.

⟿ MARY KOLADA SCOTT

NOT TECHNICALLY INCLINED

Though eminently capable,
And blessed with a good mind,
I will confess that I am not
Quite technically inclined.
I'm gifted with abilities,
And confident most days,
Yet I concede this modern flaw,
I lack tech-savvy ways.
My texts will often leave my phone
Before I want to send,
I rarely speak computerese,
My laptop's not my friend.
But I will not bemoan my lack,
Frustration will not win.
I've learned my brain can still reboot
To learn new things again.

— SUSANNE WIGGINS BUNCH

THE GEOGRAPHIC CURE

Brighten the motel room with red gladiolus
wet from rain. Know that the lake
is nearby, that the lighthouse is working.

See how the moon is a clean half
but as handsome and bright as if it were full.
Certainly your sleep will be sweet and long.

Tomorrow find the stone cottage
with the saltbox roof; there you may buy grapes
and cherries and Macintosh apples.

Wash them in the lake if you wish.
Then go wherever you like,
and drive for as long as it takes.

⌒ LONNIE HULL DUPONT

SWIMMER

The river of my courage
flows beyond the reach of
outstretched hands, yet, I hear
its current in my heart

These be turbulent times
creating eddies of anxiety
and I may lose balance along
the shoreline of my fears

There, beside a wooded bank . . .
graceful, firm-footed egret
returns, again, to search beneath
the surface for its true being

So, in must I wade, immerse myself
in the warm comfort of resolve
and swim to the distant shore . . .
confidence intact

⌒ STEPHEN KOPEL

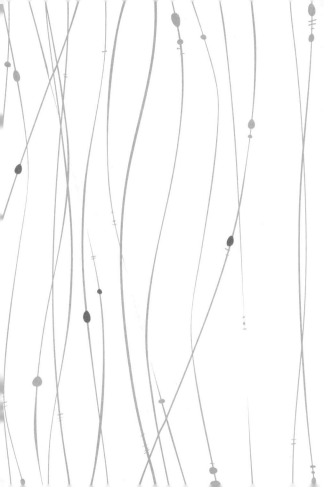

BE YOU

Embrace your uniqueness. Time is much too short to be living someone else's life.

⌒ KOBI YAMADA

The privilege of a lifetime is being who you are.

⌒ JOSEPH CAMPBELL

I read and walked for miles at night along the beach . . . searching endlessly for someone wonderful who would step out of the darkness and change my life. It never crossed my mind that that person could be me.

⌒ ANNA QUINDLEN

The minute you settle for less than you deserve, you get even less than you settled for.

⌒ MAUREEN DOWD

Your playing small does not serve the world. There is nothing enlightened about shrinking so that other people won't feel insecure around you. We are all meant to shine, as children do.

      ⌁ MARIANNE WILLIAMSON

Our deepest fear is not that we are inadequate; our deepest fear is that we are powerful beyond all measure.

      ⌁ MARIANNE WILLIAMSON

I am not a has-been. I am a will-be.

      ⌁ LAUREN BACALL

EMBRACE CHANGE

Clinging to the past is the problem.
Embracing change is the solution.

⌒ GLORIA STEINEM

seven

Finding Your Way

Put your ear down close to
your soul and listen hard.

—ANNE SEXTON

START WHERE YOU ARE

Being brave doesn't mean that you are fearless. Courage is diving through the waves, acting in spite of the fear that you feel.

When you're overwhelmed, facing a big transition, don't paralyze yourself with pressure to make The One Right Decision, as if the elusive answer you are fishing for is the only opportunity swimming in the pond. Dare to hazard a guess, to go someplace new, to choose to do things you don't know how to do.

Sometimes you just have to start walking before you can figure out where you're meant to go. Pursue what you love, what is life-giving to you as well as others.

Keep walking in hope, but don't strain toward the mirage of a finish line. Your life is always about to change. Surrender to the journey. Be open to getting your feet wet stepping into the unknown.

When you feel lost, there is no shame in stopping to ask for directions. If you've written the route on a scrap of paper and it blows out the window, don't go back and try to find it. Rest assured, you'll find your way.

⌒ EMILY RUTH HAZEL

AT LAKE CRESCENT, WASHINGTON

Suppose you find yourself
in some in-between space,
where no doors are clearly marked:
Enter here, you who would move forward.
Suppose even the currents
of your body lost their way,
and strange manifestations
disturbed the waters of your blood,
disrupted the electric currents of your heart,
beating faster than a tom-tom
in a wild warrior dance.
The chaos of your pulse and loadstones of fatigue
confuse you in contrapuntal castigations.
Then you might seek a lonely, ravaged place
where two mountains meet at Lake Crescent,
a narrow passageway between them.

Let yourself be ferried on shimmering glacial water
through a narrow portal no matter where it leads.
Know that when you pass through in-*between*
you finally find *serene*.

⌒ CHRISTINE SWANBERG

FINDING YOUR WAY

Not all those who wander are lost.

— J.R.R. TOLKIEN

Great ideas come into the world as gently as doves.
Perhaps, then, if we listen attentively, we shall hear,
amid the uproar of empires and nations, a faint
fluttering of wings, the gentle stirrings of life
and hope.

— ALBERT CAMUS

The more faithfully you listen to the voice within
you, the better you hear what is sounding outside.

— DAG HAMMARSKJÖLD

You have to leave the city of your comfort and go
into the wilderness of your intuition. What you'll
discover will be wonderful. What you'll discover
is yourself.

— ALAN ALDA

As a single footstep will not make a path on the earth, so a single thought will not make a pathway in the mind. To make a deep physical path, we walk again and again. To make a deep mental path, we must think over and over the kind of thoughts we wish to dominate our lives.

⁓ HENRY DAVID THOREAU

Not knowing when the dawn will come, I open every door.

⁓ EMILY DICKINSON

When there is no turning back, then we should concern ourselves only with the best way of going forward.

⁓ PAULO COELHO

The winds of grace blow all the time. All we need to do is set our sails.

⁓ SRI RAMAKRISHNA PARAMAHAMSA

SHATTERED PIECES

When life falls apart around us or, worse still, our
core being disintegrates, picking up the shattered
pieces isn't easy—wounded pride, broken heart,
slashed feelings—it's enough to put one foot
in front of the other each day. But this in itself
is bravery, as each step says, "Courage, do not
stumble" when we have no words. Each fake smile
means, "I will keep trying." Each tear that trickles
down, as a knife stabs our heart, whispers, "Healing
starts within."

We are not alone to face our heartache—unless
we choose to be. Others have trodden this path
before us. Take a risk. Reach out a hand and see
who grasps it. Believe it is in your power to return
the favor some day—in sweeter times—for they will
surely come.

— GWYNETH M. BLEDSOE

PUEBLO BLESSING

Hold on to what is good, even if it is a handful of earth. Hold on to what you believe, even if it is a tree which stands by itself. Hold on to what you must do, even if it is a long way from here. Hold on to life, even when it is easier letting go. Hold on to my hand, even when I have gone away from you.

⌐ AUTHOR UNKNOWN

IN SPITE OF CIRCUMSTANCES

Consider the truly happy people that you know.
I think it is unlikely that you will find that
circumstances have made them happy. They
have made themselves happy in spite of their
circumstances. . . . People can surmount what
seems to be total defeat, difficulties too great to
be borne, but it requires a capacity to readjust
endlessly to the changing conditions of life.

— ELEANOR ROOSEVELT

YES!

I don't know Who—or what—put the question, I
don't know when it was put. I don't even remember
answering. But at some moment I did answer Yes
to Someone—or Something—and from that hour
I was certain that existence is meaningful and that,
therefore, my life, in self-surrender, had a goal.

— DAG HAMMARSKJÖLD

FOLLOW YOUR BLISS

I say follow your bliss and don't be afraid, and doors will open where you didn't know they were going to be.

— JOSEPH CAMPBELL

Let yourself be silently drawn by the stronger pull of what you really love.

— RUMI (TRANSLATED BY COLEMAN BARKS)

Your time is limited, so don't waste it living someone else's life. Don't be trapped by dogma—which is living with the results of other people's thinking. Don't let the noise of others' opinions drown out your own inner voice. And most important, have the courage to follow your heart and intuition. They somehow already know what you truly want to become. Everything else is secondary.

— STEVE JOBS

LET ME BE

Today
grant me the ability to help myself
and to help others.
Let me be a light
for those who move in darkness.
Let me be a source of healing
for those that hurt.
Let me show the way
to those who are lost.
Let me forgive
those who are unforgiving.
For it is only through these actions
that I will find my own peace,
my own light,
my own intended journey
of recovery.

⌒ CORRINE DE WINTER

CHOICE BY CHOICE

Choice by choice, moment by moment,
I build the necklace of my day,
stringing together the choices that form artful living.

⟋ JULIA CAMERON

eight

Feeling Grateful

Give thanks for a little and
you will find a lot.

—HAUSA PROVERB FROM NIGERIA

JUST ANOTHER DAY

It's just another doughnut day in the universe.
I want to smash my face into flour, fluff, and
    sweetness
and forget anything that prevents me from feeling
the absolute joy of birdsong or yellow balloon
whether it be deadline or telephone line
the electronic busyness of our lives
for there are rows of tulips conspiring pink
and lovers breathless next to willow trees.
There are lilacs whispering among their twisted
    trunks
and windmills whirling through Van Gogh's ear.
There is color everywhere
and sprinkles of hope in my heart
that you will feel the freedom
of renegade rivers and the vast expanse
of starry starry nights.
Connect the dots, the body of water
between us, this great flood of love
that seeps through and beyond the earth.

    ⌒ TERRI GLASS

SUNDAY'S THEME

In the stories I return to, people love each other
indirectly. Offering coins, their moonlit
faces. Not receiving too much credit.
Like the man at work today who answered
"How are you?" with "Blessed." I thought,
that's not an answer to the question.
Afterward, I spent the day remembering:
I'm alive and breathing, drinking tea
with cinnamon. All day that was beautiful.
Later afternoon, the crew team spuming
wings of mist beyond me on the Mississippi,
each man's stroke and strain of back
a promise to his boat-fellows, a steady line
to shore. Someone else can speak about
the heart of love. I'll keep its faithful
offerings. Blooming sky this evening,
and footsteps at the door.

⌒ EMILY K. BRIGHT

BE THANKFUL

Be thankful that you don't already have everything
you desire. If you did, what would there be to look
forward to?

Be thankful when you don't know something
For it gives you the opportunity to learn.

Be thankful for the difficult times.
During those times you grow.

Be thankful for your limitations
Because they give you opportunities for
improvement.

Be thankful for each new challenge
Because it will build your strength and character.

Be thankful for your mistakes
They will teach you valuable lessons.

Be thankful when you're tired and weary
Because it means you've made a difference.

It is easy to be thankful for the good things.
A life of rich fulfillment comes to those who are
also thankful for the setbacks.

Gratitude can turn a negative into a positive.

Find a way to be thankful for your troubles
and they can become your blessings.

⌒ AUTHOR UNKNOWN

BREAK IN THE GRAY

Another winter day,
dismal and gray, until
a gold finch and a cardinal
glide in and land on the runway
around the bird feeder
just outside my kitchen window.
They peck at the bird seed
then fly away, leaving
me to wonder
if the birds just happened by
or if they were sent
as gifts of beauty and joy
to lift despondent spirits.

⌒ SANDRA H. BOUNDS

BEYOND THE RAINBOWS

When you take away all the colors of life
distill things down to dark and light,
black and white

Take note, the beauty in the delineation,
the contrast
the images, stark, defined.

The glory of a simple line
etched into the frost of a windowpane

The angled tree branch, crooked
arched, raised toward heaven.

∾ DARLENE MOORE BERG

SATURDAY MORNING

Sunlight grazes
my face too early,

meadowlark committing
to good cheer warbles

atop chimney, hinting
of life's small, sweet things—

ah—sun-dried sheets
under my nose.

∽ KATE ROBINSON

GRATITUDE ATTITUDE

The world and I grow weary,
so it is easy to wake up on the wrong side
    of the bed,
to see my chipped china cup as half empty,
feel myself small against the curtain of sky.

Why cheat myself with adages passed down
when I can take that cup,
fill it half full with pungent soil,
plant a bright yellow marigold,
set it on the worn white wicker table
over which the lilac blooms,
where early morning birds sing in the day
and I hold the joy of hands dusted with dirt.

— JOYCE LOMBARD

PEACE BEGINS WITHIN

Sometimes it's the little things that mean the most: the song of a bird, a warm breeze blowing through the trees, a friendly voice on the other end of a telephone, a note written by a friend to us when we need encouragement, the wag of a dog's tail as we come home from a hard day at work. These things are intangible—we cannot put a price tag on what they mean to us or how they help us to feel abiding peace even in the midst of turmoil. When I am tempted to lose control and get angry or bitter, I must remember the things which make me happy, and become peaceful within. No matter what the outward appearances, I can always return to these things, and feel the joy that comes from them.

Today I am thankful for the little things that bring peace from within.

⌐ HEATHER PARKINS

THINK OF ALL THE BEAUTY

Think of all the beauty
still left around
and be happy.

⚬— ANNE FRANK

TULIP

I watched its first green push
through bare dirt, where the builders
had dropped boards, shingles, plaster—
killing everything.
I could not recall what grew there,
what returned each spring,
but the leaves looked tulip,
and one morning it arrived,
a scarlet slash against the aluminum siding.

Mornings, on the way to my car,
I bow to the still bell
of its closed petals; evenings
it greets me, light ringing
at the end of my driveway.

Sometimes I kneel
to stare into the yellow throat,
count the black tongues,
stroke the firm red mouth.
It opens and closes my days.
It has made me weak with love,
this god I didn't know I needed.

— PENNY HARTER

REFLECTIONS ON GRATITUDE

It is not how much we have,
but how much we enjoy it
that makes for happiness.

⌒ AUTHOR UNKNOWN

You simply will not be the same person two months from now after consciously giving thanks each day for the abundance that exists in your life. And you will have set in motion an ancient spiritual law: the more you have and are grateful for, the more will be given you.

⌒ SARAH BAN BREATHNACH

God gave you a gift of 86,400 seconds today. Have you used one to say "thank you"?

⌒ WILLIAM ARTHUR WARD

If the only prayer you said in your whole life was "thank you," that would suffice.

⌒ MEISTER ECKHART

Darkness deserves gratitude. It is the alleluia point at which we learn to understand that all growth does not take place in the sunlight.

⌒ JOAN CHITTISTER

A grateful mind is a great mind which eventually attracts to itself great things.

⌒ ERIC BUTTERWORTH

Happiness cannot be traveled to, owned, earned, worn, or consumed. Happiness is the spiritual experience of living every minute with love, grace, and gratitude.

⌒ DENIS WAITLEY

A DAY WILL COME WHEN . . .

Warm rays of sunlight
will scintillate your chilled skin,
And a mountain-fresh breeze will make you
inhale again just for pleasure.
Rustling leaves will soothe you with their melody,
And a pansy's dappled face will make you stop
and stare at Nature's wonder.

When that day comes,
You will know—
The suffocating void has passed
        and you are once again Whole.

— MARY A. BECKER

nine

Reflections

Joy is not in things;
it is in us.

—RICHARD WAGNER

REFLECTIONS ON JOY

Joy is what happens when we allow ourselves to recognize how good things are.

— MARIANNE WILLIAMSON

You increase your joy by increasing the pure joy of others.

— TORKOM SARAYDARIAN

Friendship improves happiness and abates misery, by the doubling of our joy and the dividing of our grief.

— MARCUS TULLIUS CICERO

The joy that you give to others is the joy that comes back to you.

— JOHN GREENLEAF WHITTIER

HAPPINESS

My happiness grows in direct proportion [to]
my acceptance and in inverse proportion to my
expectations.

⟋ MICHAEL J. FOX

There is a direct correlation between the level of
happiness in one's life and the amount of silliness
they allow into it.

⟋ CURLY GIRL DESIGN

Most people are about as happy as they make up
their minds to be.

⟋ ABRAHAM LINCOLN

I am more and more convinced that our happiness
or our unhappiness depends far more on the way
we meet the events of life than on the nature of
those events themselves.

⟋ WILHELM VON HUMBOLDT

THAT'S WHAT FRIENDS ARE FOR

Weary, tired, frustrated
I've hit the wall.
Drag myself to meet my friends.

The food is tasty,
The music prods my spirit
Smiles, laughter, lifting me
To a place where I can breathe again
Where I can find peace again
Where I can be myself again.

⌒ NANCY ENGLER

DEEP GRATITUDE

At times our own light goes out and is rekindled by a spark from another person. Each of us has cause to think with deep gratitude of those who have lighted the flame within us.

— ALBERT SCHWEITZER

FRIENDSHIPS

Each friend represents a world in us, a world possibly not born until they arrive, and it is only by this meeting that a new world is born. — ANAÏS NIN

Friends are to be cherished in all stages of life as they bring joy and comfort, laughter and tears. Through their struggles we redefine our faith and beliefs. Through our struggles we gain new perspectives and support.

May we expand our world of friendship to become invisible hands that guide or open vessels to receive a new vision.

— JUDY ACKLEY BROWN

Friendship doubles joy
and cuts grief in half.

⌐ FRANCIS BACON

FOR CONTEMPLATION

One must have chaos within to give birth to a dancing star.

— FRIEDRICH NIETZSCHE

I will love the light for it shows me the way, yet I will endure the darkness for it shows me the stars.

— OG MANDINO

There comes a point in your life when you realize: Who matters, who never did, who won't anymore . . . and who always will. So, don't worry about people from your past, there's a reason why they didn't make it to your future.

— AUTHOR UNKNOWN

When things are bad, we take comfort in the thought that they could always be worse. And when they are, we find hope in the thought that things are so bad they have to get better.

— MALCOLM FORBES

Between stimulus and response there is a space.
In that space is our power to choose our response.
In our response lies our growth and our freedom.

— VIKTOR FRANKL

Our continual mistake is that we do not
concentrate upon the present day, the actual hour,
of our life: we live in the past or in the future; we
are continually expecting the coming of some
special moment when our life will unfold itself in
its full significance. And we do not notice that life is
flowing like water through our fingers.

— FATHER ALEXANDER ELCHANINOV

The truth is—everything counts.
Everything.
Everything we do and everything we say.
Everything helps or hurts.
Everything adds to or
takes away from someone else.

— COUNTEE CULLEN

SOLE SOLUTION

As a young woman, I wore four-inch heels. Now I can't look at stiletto heels on shoe racks without flinching at the thought of pinched, aching, and unbalanced feet.

As I aged, I settled for two-inch heels. As those also became precarious, I suffered anguish at the prospect of throwing away my pumps. One night, I sat with a favorite pair of worn-out heels in my lap, trying to convince myself to toss them in the trash. Suddenly, I grabbed my nearby sketchbook. I did a quick watercolor and ink sketch of them and added the following tribute:

> "Pretty soon,
> they'll take away
> my pretty shoes
> but I won't be
> defeated."

I felt I had paid homage to the young woman I had been and the shoes that had carried me this far.

I discarded the heels, but I decided that I wouldn't pitch any more shoes until I had honored them in paint.

When I mentioned this to other women, they were delighted with the idea. I painted acrylic paintings of my favorite shoes. Other women brought me their favorite shoes—red-soled Christian Louboutin heels, cowboy boots, Italian slings, flip-flops, and fierce leather boots worthy of a rock star. I painted girls' baby shoes. I exhibited some of my paintings at an art show, and five paintings sold the first day. Women approached me to immortalize their precious shoes with commissioned paintings.

I seldom wear heels now and have found a wide selection of flats—fun, classy, trendy and comfortable. I'm still well-heeled but more grounded. I've learned that loss can lead to revelation and rewards. In the long run, it doesn't matter what you wear on your feet, as long as you keep moving.

∼ MARY KOLADA SCOTT

MORE

I'm not sure how much more there is
than the promise of five small eggs
laid by a phoebe inside a carport.
One day, some of them will hatch
or none of them or maybe two or three,
and perhaps I will be there to see them
fly into the meadow beyond the yard
or maybe they will strike out alone,
when nobody is looking, not me, not you,
and life will go on, no more sacred,
no less tragic, simply what it is right now:
a nest of phoebes with five small eggs
as fragile as any hope I can ever have
and as open to the possibility of flight
as little birds about to hatch can be.

⌁ FELICIA MITCHELL

REMEMBERING

the sun is setting
behind the hills
dense with trees

on the other side
not far from here
the ocean is still bright

    another lesson
    in remembering
        (everything is relative
    of course)

this tiny planet
orbits a mighty star
always shining somewhere
        on us

            light always
        in us

    VIRGINIA BARRETT

UNEXPECTED BLESSINGS

Small graces come to us in unexpected places.
Many great things are born from dark places.

⌒ CORRINE DE WINTER

When we lose one blessing, another is often, most
unexpectedly, given in its place.

⌒ C. S. LEWIS

A few years' experience will convince us that
those things which at the time they happened we
regarded as our greatest misfortunes have proved
our greatest blessings.

⌒ GEORGE MASON

For everything you have missed, you have gained
something else; and for everything you gain, you
lose something else.

⌒ RALPH WALDO EMERSON

NATURE'S EXAMPLE

How easily Nature overcomes every obstacle.
The tiny ant walks over the stone.
The roots of the tree embrace the rocks in the soil.
The river flows around every log and boulder in
    its way.
Like Nature, we should adapt to life's circumstances,
overcoming them with patience and enthusiasm.

— AMMA

THE BEST REMEDY

The best remedy for those who are afraid, lonely, or unhappy is to go outside, somewhere where they can be quite alone with the heavens, nature, and God.

⟜ ANNE FRANK

CONSTANT CHANGE

Constant change
is the nature of the world.
Every moment, every single thing
is changing.

⌐ AMMA

TAKING RISKS

All the world is a very narrow bridge, and the most
important thing is not to fear at all.

⤳ REBBE NACHMAN OF BRESLOV

The greatest mistake you can make in life is to be
continually fearing you will make one.

⤳ ELBERT HUBBARD

It is impossible to live without failing at
something—unless you live so cautiously that you
might as well not have lived at all, in which case
you have failed by default.

⤳ J. K. ROWLING

And the day came when the risk to remain tight
in a bud was more painful than the risk it took
to blossom.

⤳ ANAÏS NIN

There are many ways we can grow as human beings but there are only two universal experiences: Either we are broken open, or we willfully shed what isn't working in our lives.

⟶ MARK NEPO

With each victory, no matter how great the cost or how agonizing at the time, there comes increased confidence and strength to help meet the next fear. . . . You must make yourself succeed. You must do the thing you think you cannot do.

⟶ ELEANOR ROOSEVELT

To get through the hardest journey we need take only one step at a time, but we must keep on stepping.

⟶ CHINESE PROVERB

FROM AN ANGEL AT MIDNIGHT

Do you not realize that your life here
Is so small in the scheme of things?
You get frustrated and depressed from small earthly
    things
when they do not really matter in the big picture.
What matters is that you live as fully as you can,
that you love as fully as you are able to—
that you are kind and give of your heart to others
who have much less.
I tell you this now, with a wisdom
beyond what you may be capable of grasping.
This life here is not the end—it is the beginning.
When you look back on this world,
and this life from beyond
you will laugh, and realize
that all these incidents and impossibilities
were temporary lessons that you did your best at—
and that it was good enough.

You did your best in these impossible, earthly
   situations.
No one expected more. No one.
You are too hard on yourself.

It's okay,
We are human beings, trying to BE.
And that is enough.

— CORRINE DE WINTER

KEEP LEARNING

As long as you live,
keep learning how to live.

⟳— SENECA

ten

Inspiration

The best is yet to be.

—ROBERT BROWNING

THE WORLD HAS NEED OF YOU

everything here
seems to need us

⤚ RAINER MARIA RILKE

I can hardly imagine it
as I walk to the lighthouse, feeling the ancient
prayer of my arms swinging
in counterpoint to my feet.
Here I am, suspended
between the sidewalk and twilight,
the sky dimming so fast it seems alive.
What if you felt the invisible
tug between you and everything?
A boy on a bicycle rides by,
his white shirt open, flaring
behind him like wings.

It's a hard time to be human. We know too much
and too little. Does the breeze need us?
The cliffs? The gulls?
If you've managed to do one good thing,
the ocean doesn't care.
But when Newton's apple fell toward the earth,
the earth, ever so slightly, fell
toward the apple.

⌒ ELLEN BASS

ALWAYS, JOY EMERGING

over every blade of grass, an angel bends,
whispering, grow, grow.

⌒ AN OLD JEWISH PROVERB

Always, something absolutely remarkable
is happening.
How, for example, moonlight
rings its gauzy rainbow
into the night sky, brightens the coal-blue blackness.

Every time I consider the impossibility
of everything I know, I am reminded of
how much I do not understand

and marvel again at that sudden rush of time
of Winter flowing into Spring,
of how buds and seeds understand,
despite the cold and snow,

when their time has come,
how they know to listen when
their angels whisper, "grow, grow."

∽ MICHAEL S. GLASER

FIND WONDER EVERYWHERE

And above all, watch with glittering eyes the whole world around you because the greatest secrets are always hidden in the most unlikely places.

— ROALD DAHL

It is a glorious privilege to live, to know, to act, to listen, to behold, to love. To look up at the blue summer sky; to see the sun sink slowly beyond the line of the horizon; to watch the worlds come twinkling into view, first one by one, and the myriads that no [person] can count, and lo! the universe is white with them; and you and I are here.

— MARCO MORROW

One of life's most fulfilling moments occurs in the split-second when the familiar is suddenly transformed into the dazzling aura of the profoundly new.

— EDWARD B. LINDAMAN

Observe the wonders as they occur around you. Don't claim them. Feel the artistry moving through you, and be silent.

— RUMI (TRANSLATED BY COLEMAN BARKS)

TU WI'S CONSIDERS APRIL SUNLIGHT

Tu Wi's is an imaginary poet of the S'ung Dynasty (960-1260)

Some cook in the sky must be ladling it out,
pouring liquid gold from her copper saucepan,
basting the meadow in hollandaise.
Where it drips: buttercups, dandelions,
butter & eggs. Where it splashes: forsythia,
daffodils, tulips. After this long hard winter,
I reach out my arms, lift my face to the sky.
Fry me, sunny side up, on spring's hot griddle;
clarify me, anoint me, in your lavish lemon light.

∽ BARBARA CROOKER

IT'S A GREAT LIFE

I like living. I have sometimes been wildly despairing, acutely miserable, racked with sorrow, but through it all I still know quite certainly that just to *be* alive is a grand thing.

⟋ AGATHA CHRISTIE

Life, for all its agonies of despair and loss and guilt, is exciting and beautiful, amusing and artful and endearing, full of liking and love, at times a poem and a high adventure, at times noble and at times very gay; and whatever (if anything) is to come after it—we shall not have this life again.

⟋ ROSE MACAULAY

Life is a great and wondrous mystery, and the only thing we know that we have for sure is what is right here right now. Don't miss it.

⟋ LEO BUSCAGLIA

SERENDIPITY

I scribbled down a prayer the other day,
a relentless journey from my heart
to my hand, when I wadded it up
like a Kleenex, stashed it deep down
into my jeans' back pocket. But

without thinking, I threw those pants
into my Maytag for a wash, then dry,
and before putting them away that night,
I shook them roughly to bypass ironing.

A confetti of words danced in the air,
rainbow colored morsels of gratitude
and heartfelt requests. Expecting them
to fall unheard to the ground, I was
amazed to see them spiral upwards.

⌒ SUSAN ROGERS NORTON

YOUR DESTINY

Maybe you feel like your destiny was written the day you were born, and you ought to just rein in your hopes and scale back your dreams. But if any of you are thinking that way, I'm here to tell you, stop it. Don't ever scale back your dreams. And don't ever set limits on what you can achieve. And don't think for one single moment that your destiny is out of your hands, because no one's in control of your destiny but you.

⟋ MICHELLE OBAMA

YOU ONLY LIVE ONCE

So make it worth your while.
Be fearless, true to yourself
and give everything you have.
Live for today and take care of the people you love,
and those that love you will do the same.

Let go of anything that is negative
and holding you down,
and always search for the positive
that will help you fly.
Don't waste time worrying about a life
that is limited, because everything that challenges
your spirit makes you stronger.

Keep moving toward all the good that you can find
because the reward for a life that is lived
to the fullest, is a life that is extraordinary
and filled with purpose.

Explore every exciting opportunity
and each open door.
Don't be held back by what you are unsure about.
Forever pursue what your heart is craving because
it will always lead you to your best self.

This is the only life you have so always
reach for the best.
Don't let anyone deter you from being fiercely
happy and content.
As long as you come from a place of
honesty and truth, you will deserve all the goodness
that finds its way to you.

Remember to listen, touch, hold, and contribute.
And never forget to give, respect, love, and embrace.
Your life can be genuinely amazing
if you just live it every day!

— LORI EBERHARDY

THE IMPACT OF ATTITUDE

The longer I live, the more I realize the impact of attitude on life. Attitude, to me, is more important than facts. It is more important than the past, the education, the money, than circumstances, than failure, than successes, than what other people think or say or do. The remarkable thing is we have a choice everyday regarding the attitude we will embrace for that day. We cannot change our past. We cannot change the fact that people will act in a certain way. We cannot change the inevitable. The only thing we can do is play on the one string we have, and that is our attitude. I am convinced that life is 10% what happens to me and 90% of how I react to it. And so it is with you. We are in charge of our attitudes.

⌒ CHARLES SWINDOLL

Good Little Reminders

This moment only
is all there is.

—JANINE CANAN

MIRACLES

Little miracles come into our lives, not on huge
bolts of lightning, but on gentle beams of light,
love, and hope.

⤚DAN ZADRA

When we pray, we are speaking to God. When a
miracle happens, God is speaking to us.

⤚AUTHOR UNKNOWN

You can hope for a miracle in your life, or you can
realize that your life is the miracle.

⤚ROBERT BRAULT

Prepare yourself for miracles today.

⤚ROBERT HOLDEN

INNER PEACE

Tension is who you think you should be. Relaxation is who you are.

— CHINESE PROVERB

Within you there is a stillness, a haven to which you can withdraw at any time and be at home there.

— HERMANN HESSE

Though we travel the world over to find the beautiful, we must carry it with us or we will not find it.

— RALPH WALDO EMERSON

life is full
just breathe
deep

— SHERYL L. NELMS

FIND DELIGHT EVERY DAY

Mix a little foolishness with your serious plans. It is lovely to be silly at the right moment.

⌒ HORACE

Each day, and the living of it, has to be a conscious creation in which discipline and order are relieved with some play and foolishness.

⌒ MAY SARTON

It is essential to our well-being, and to our lives, that we play and enjoy life. Every single day, do something that makes your heart sing.

⌒ MARCIA WIEDER

Find the thing that stirs your heart and make room for it. Life is about the development of self to the point of unbridled joy.

⌒ JOAN CHITTISTER

THIS DAY

Let me be:
Ready at your beckoning
Faithful on my journey
Constant in my efforts
To be Your song.

⁓ MARY LENORE QUIGLEY

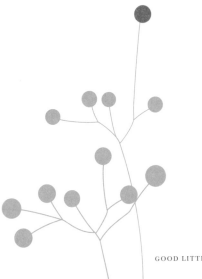

TODAY

In the entire history of the universe, let alone in your own history, there has never been another day just like today, and there will never be another just like it again. Today is the point to which all your yesterdays have been leading since the hour of your birth. It is the point from which all your tomorrows will proceed until the hour of your death. If you were aware of how precious today is, you could hardly live through it. Unless you are aware of how precious it is, you can hardly be said to be living at all.

— FREDERICK BUECHNER

LIFE'S JOURNEY

Your journey has molded you for your greater good, and it was exactly what it needed to be. Don't think you've lost time. There is no short-cutting to life. It took each and every situation you have encountered to bring you to the now. And now is right on time.

∾ ASHA TYSON

Life isn't about how you survived the storm . . . it's about how you danced in the rain.

∾ REGINA BRETT

How we spend our days is, of course, how we spend our lives.

∾ ANNIE DILLARD

The beautiful journey of today can only begin when we learn to let go of yesterday.

∾ STEVE MARABOLI

OUR ATTITUDE

We cannot choose how many years we will live, but we can choose how much life those years will have.

We cannot control the beauty of our face, but we can control the expression on it.

We cannot control life's difficult moments but we can choose to make life less difficult.

We cannot control the negative atmosphere of the world, but we can control the atmosphere of our minds.

Too often we try to choose and control things we cannot.

Too seldom we choose to control what we can . . . our attitude.

— JOHN C. MAXWELL

LIVE EACH DAY

Write it on your heart that every day is the best day of the year.

— RALPH WALDO EMERSON

Let today be a day where you take nothing for granted. For life is fleeting, fragile, and precious, and can change on a whim. Say all the things you really want to say to your loved ones today, say the things you would regret should they pass on and your words remain unspoken.

— JACKSON KIDDARD

We have only this moment, sparkling like a star in our hand . . . and melting like a snowflake. Let us use it now before it is too late.

— MARIE BEYNON LYONS RAY

My deepest belief is that living as if you are dying sets us free.

— ANNE LAMOTT

Stuff your eyes with wonder, live as if you'd drop dead in ten seconds. See the world. It's more fantastic than any dream made or paid for in factories.

⌒ RAY BRADBURY

If you live each day as if it was your last, someday you'll most certainly be right.

⌒ STEVE JOBS

There are only two days in the year that nothing can be done. One is called yesterday and the other is called tomorrow, so today is the right day to love, believe, do, and mostly live.

⌒ THE DALAI LAMA

Amazing how we can light tomorrow with today.

⌒ ELIZABETH BARRETT BROWNING

BE KIND

It's hard to feel bad about yourself when you're doing something good for someone else.

⟋ JOHN C. MAXWELL

Those who are the happiest are those who do the most for others.

⟋ BOOKER T. WASHINGTON

In life you can never be too kind or too fair. Everyone you meet is carrying a heavy load. When you go through your day expressing kindness and courtesy to all you meet, you leave behind a feeling of warmth and good cheer, and you help alleviate the burdens everyone is struggling with.

⟋ BRIAN TRACY

Happiness is not so much in having as sharing. We make a living by what we get, but we make a life by what we give.

⟋ NORMAN MACEWEN

Let no one ever come to you without leaving better and happier.

— MOTHER TERESA

We all have the power to give away love, to love other people. And if we do so, we change the kind of person we are, and we change the kind of world we live in.

— HAROLD KUSHNER

You will find, as you look back upon your life, that the moments when you really lived are the moments when you have done things in the spirit of love.

— HENRY DRUMMOND

The best way to find yourself is to lose yourself in the service of others.

— MAHATMA GANDHI

GOOD ADVICE

Beginning today, treat everyone you meet as if they were going to be dead by midnight. Extend to them all the care, kindness, and understanding you can muster, and do it with no thought of any reward. Your life will never be the same again.

⌒ OG MANDINO

The secret of happiness is this: Let your interests be as wide as possible, and let your reactions to the things and persons that interest you be as far as possible friendly rather than hostile.

⌒ BERTRAND RUSSELL

Surround yourself with people who know your worth. You don't need too many people to be happy, just a few real ones who appreciate you for exactly who you are.

⌒ AUTHOR UNKNOWN

Talking about our problems has become our greatest addiction. Break the habit—talk about your joys.

           RITA SCHIANO

The real things haven't changed. It is still best to be honest and truthful; to make the most of what we have; to be happy with simple pleasures; and have courage when things go wrong.

           LAURA INGALLS WILDER

Do what you can, with what you have, where you are.

           THEODORE ROOSEVELT

Live simply, expect little, give much.

           NORMAN VINCENT PEALE

Forgive, forget, and forge ahead.

           AUTHOR UNKNOWN

GOOD QUESTIONS

One way to open your eyes is to ask yourself,
"What if I had never seen this before? What if I
knew I would never see it again?"

            ○— RACHEL CARSON

Each string of a wind harp responds with a
different note to the same breeze. What activity
makes you personally resonate most strongly, most
deeply, with the wind of the Spirit that blows where
it wills?

            ○— DAVID STEINDL-RAST

Which is more artistic: to make an imaginative work of art or to live an imaginative life?

— KAZUAKI TANAHASHI

If you aren't making at least one person smile a day, what are you doing?

— MICHAEL NEPHEW
(excerpted from "Homeless in Seattle" Facebook page)

ANGELS ARE AMONG US

There are angels among us. You may have
encountered one recently: a nurse answering a
patient's call, a busy clerk helping you find just what
you need, a smile from a small child, a thoughtful
stranger opening a door for you, an anonymous
donor bringing unexpected financial relief. Look
for angels around every corner. Seen and unseen,
they are there to give your soul a lift and offer a
helping hand. When you hear the sound of wings
brushing past, remember that angels are watching
over you.

⏤ CANDY PAULL

BREATH

In the stillness
of this breath
I can take comfort
in knowing I am
part of something
greater than myself.

— JOAN NOËLDECHEN

IT'S A WONDERFUL LIFE!

Oh, my friend, it is not what they take away from
you that counts,
it is what you do with what you have left.

— HUBERT H. HUMPHREY

How beautiful it is to be alive!

— HENRY SEPTIMUS SUTTON

And, I think to myself, what a wonderful world.

— LOUIS ARMSTRONG

AUTHOR INDEX

PERMISSIONS AND ACKNOWLEDGMENTS

Grateful acknowledgment is made to the authors and publishers for the use of the following material. Every effort has been made to contact original sources. If notified, the publishers will be pleased to rectify an omission in future editions.

Joan Marie Arbogast for "Ready or Not . . ." and "Steadfast Hope." www.joanmariearbogast.com

Coleman Barks for "Let yourself be silently drawn" and "Observe the wonders" from *The Essential Rumi*, translated by Coleman Barks and John Moyne. Copyright © 1995 by Coleman Barks. Published by HarperSanFrancisco. Permission to reprint granted by Coleman Barks. www.colemanbarks.com

Virginia Barrett for "Remembering." www.virginiabarrett.com

Ellen Bass for "Relax" and "The World Has Need of You" from *Like a Beggar*. Copyright © 2014 by Ellen Bass. Reprinted with the permission of The Permissions Company, Inc. on behalf of Copper Canyon Press, www.coppercanyonpress.org, www.ellenbass.com

Jean Nicole Bass for "Begin."

Mary A. Becker for "A Day Will Come When . . ."

Darlene Moore Berg for "Beyond the Rainbows." www.darlenemb.wordpress.com

Gwyneth M. Bledsoe for "Shattered Pieces." www.gwynethbledsoe.com

Sandra H. Bounds for "Break in the Gray."

Emily K. Bright for "Sunday's Theme."
www.emilykbright.com

Judy Ackley Brown for "Friendships."

Susanne Wiggins Bunch for "Not Technically Inclined."

Laura Byrnes for "When Life Takes Guts."

Janine Canan for "The Treasure" and "This moment only."
www.janinecanan.com

Lauren Kate Ciminera for "Sometimes your struggles."

Sally Clark for "Faith." www.sallyclark.info

Barbara Crooker for "Tu Wi's Considers April Sunlight."
www.barbaracrooker.com

Jill Frances Davis for "Friends Indeed."

Barbara Davis-Pyles for "In Darkness."

Corrine De Winter for "If you have forgotten," "Sanctuary,"
"Let Me Be," "Small graces come," and "From an Angel at
Midnight." www.corrinedewinter.com

Lonnie Hull DuPont for "The Geographic Cure."

Lori Eberhardy for "You Only Live Once," "Breathing
Between the Lines," and "Great Expectations."

Nancy Engler for "That's What Friends Are for" and
"The Sun's Touch."

Ruth Fogelman for "Just." www.jerusalemlives.weebly.com

Nancy Lynch Gibson for "Jump!"

Michael S. Glaser for "Always, Joy Emerging."
www.michaelsglaser.com

Terri Glass for "Just Another Day." www.terriglass.com

Ingrid Goff-Maidoff for "Sometimes We Must Let the
Weeping Come." www.ingridgoffmaidoff.com

Penny Harter for "Tulip" from *Turtle Blessing*. Copyright © 1996 by Penny Harter. Reprinted with the permission of the author. www.2hweb.net/penhart

C. David Hay for "Angels."

Emily Ruth Hazel for "Start Where You Are." www.facebook.com/emilyruthhazel

Laura Jean Judson for "Confidence."

Susan Koefod for "Permission Granted." www.susankoefod.com

Stephen Kopel for "Swimmer."

Arlene Gay Levine for "Each step is the journey." www.arlenegaylevine.com

Judith A. Lindberg for "Be Kind to Yourself."

Nancy Tupper Ling for "Shower me." www.nancytupperling.com

Joyce Lombard for "Gratitude Attitude."

Jill N. MacGregor for "If you can remember."

Arlene L. Mandell for "Troubles Like Weeds."

Mata Amritanandamayi Center and Janine Canan for "Constant Change" and "Nature's Example" by Amma. "Constant Change" appears on p. 61 of *Garland of Love* by Mata Amritanandamayi, edited by Janine Canan. Copyright © 2013 by Mata Amritanandamayi Center. "Nature's Example" appears on p. 33 of *Messages from Amma: In the Language of the Heart*, edited by Janine Canan. Copyright © 2004 by Janine Canan. Published by Celestial Arts. Permission to reprint both selections granted by Mata Amritanandamayi Center and Janine Canan. www.amma.org, www. janinecanan.com

Barb Mayer for "Rebirth." www.barbmayer.com

Felicia Mitchell for "More."

Sheryl L. Nelms for "Life is full."

Joan Noëldechen for "Breath."
www.myspace.com/writingspaces

Sudie Nostrand for "Self-Embrace."

Heather Parkins for "Peace Begins Within."

Candy Paull for "Angel Are Among Us."
www.candypaull.com

Mary Lenore Quigley for "This Day." www.q2ink.com

DeMar Regier for "14 Little Ways to Beat the Blues."

Kate Robinson for "Saturday Morning."
http://katerwriter.tripod.com

Mary Kolada Scott for "The Art of Joy," "Sole Solution,"
and "Road Back to Joy." www.marykoladascott.com

Sherri Waas Shunfenthal for "Life Is Messy."

Christine Swanberg for "Embrace Uncertainty As a Cloud"
and "At Lake Crescent, Washington."

Edie Weinstein for "Elevator Story." www.liveinjoy.org

Barbara Younger for "Just Breathe," "Just Over Yonder,"
and "Send Out Some Joy." www.friendfortheride.com

ABOUT THE AUTHOR

June Cotner is the author or editor of thirty books, including the best-selling *Graces*, *Bedside Prayers*, and *Dog Blessings*. Her books altogether have sold nearly one million copies. June's latest love and avocation is giving presentations on adopting prisoner-trained shelter dogs. In 2011, she adopted Indy, a chocolate lab/Doberman mix (a LabraDobie!), from the Freedom Tails program at Stafford Creek Corrections Center in Aberdeen, Washington. June works with Indy daily to build on the wonderful obedience skills he mastered in the program. She and Indy have appeared on the television shows *AM Northwest* in Portland, Oregon, and *New Day Northwest* in Seattle.

A graduate of the University of California at Berkeley, June is the mother of two grown children and lives in Poulsbo, Washington with her husband. Her hobbies include yoga, hiking, and playing with her two grandchildren.

For more information, please visit June's Web site at www.JuneCotner.com.